IMAGES
of England

NEWQUAY

Sarah Teague Husband was born in Newquay in 1850 to William and Mary Ann Husband. Her father was a labourer and her mother a dressmaker. She went on to teach at Brownston Mixed School at Modbury in Devon in 1874. Her hobbies included collecting and mounting seaweed, making miniature furniture and painting in oils. As a girl she often rowed in local regattas and loved to boast of the prizes she won. She is most famous for her book of recollections of *Old Newquay*, first published in 1923.

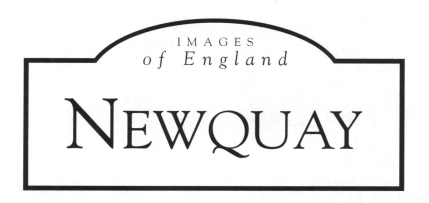

IMAGES
of England

NEWQUAY

Compiled by
Joyce Greenham and Sheila Harper

TEMPUS

First published 1999
Reprinted 1999
Copyright © Joyce Greenham and Sheila Harper, 1999

Tempus Publishing Limited
The Mill, Brimscombe Port,
Stroud, Gloucestershire, GL5 2QG

ISBN 0 7524 1827 0

Typesetting and origination by
Tempus Publishing Limited
Printed in Great Britain by
Midway Clark Printing, Wiltshire

To the people of Newquay

Newquay Lifeboat Day, *c.* 1900. This was an exciting event. Accompanied by a brass band the boat was paraded through town, drawn on its carriage by heavy horses. Stopping at the Great Western, Victoria and Central Hotels, its occupants, summer concert parties and local singers provided entertainment from aboard the vessel.

Contents

River Gannel, 1886. The Gannel is listed as a Cornish port in the thirteenth century, carrying on a brisk trade with Wales and Ireland. The 1700s saw it as a place 'where much fish and fowl are caught and many ships frequent the place for trade'. In the eighteenth century, Welsh coal for the Truro Smelting Works was unshipped at Penpol or Trevemper, and carried there along packhorse tracks. By the nineteenth century there was a shipyard at Tregunnel and barges still carried goods up to Trevemper. The buildings of Pentire Farm can be seen on the left.

Introduction

The magnificent cliffs, miles of beaches, two estuaries, farm land, minerals, shell fish, sea fish and safe havens for seafarers have always attracted visitors. In Late Mesolithic times, hunter gatherers, following the red deer herds off Bodmin Moor, spent their summers here. They left their flint tools and stone axes and waste along the high places. Settlers followed, founding homesteads and farms around the sea bent rivers. Later Bronze Age ritual practices led to many great burial mounds being built, still standing proud on headlands and cliffs. Streaming for tin and iron mining and iron smelting meant trade with far places. Christians from over the sea found a welcome, and formed religious communities up the sheltered estuaries and gave their names to our parishes of Crantock and St Columb Minor. An ecclesiastical college followed at Crantock. Local manors featured in the Domesday Book; Crantock, Cargoll, Lanherne, Tolcarne, Treninnick, Treloy and Rialton, which later became the country home of Vyvyan, Prior of Bodmin and titular Bishop of Megara. Important medieval trackways from Penpol Creek on the River Gannel allowed trade through the heart of Cornwall to and from Truro and Penryn. The Catholic Arundells were at Treloy and Lanherne, made rich by successful marriages, and much land in the area was owned by the Church and then the Crown, after the time of Henry VIII.

What has all this got to do with the 'Newquay' of today? The Manor of Tewyn Blustry, in St Columb Minor had a small cove, a landing place for fishing vessels. In 1439 permission was sought to build a 'keye' there. By 1571, in the Arundell papers, there is a mention of a ship arriving at Newekaye, near a little village called Towen Blystra. A fish market was also present. In the next 200 years mention is made of rebuilding the quay, free trading in the area and fish cellars in operation, as well as the Manor changing hands. The villagers carried on fishing, farming and mining. They travelled to Crantock or St Columb Minor to go to church, be buried and educated. A few rich visitors came for the bracing sea air. The River Gannel was being used to offload goods, such as coal, from shipping berthed there, for transport to Trevemper by barge and distribution around the area.

The impetus for change from a tiny fishing village, at Towan Blystra, into one of Britain's foremost holiday resorts, Newquay, occurred when Richard Lomax became Lord of the Manor. He began to develop his holdings but died in 1837, so the Manor was put up for sale again. Newquay was by then a flourishing town, with nearly 100 acres of rich fertile orchard, meadow and pasture and 70 acres of sheep walk. There was a bigger pier capable of taking ships up to 700 tons burthen and dues available from the local pilchard fishing industry. The Newquay Silver and Lead Mine was in production. A railway had been projected, connecting one side of Cornwall with the other, which could stop the necessity of taken goods around the dangerous seas off Land End. There were rents from two inns, the coastguard houses, a boat building yard, villager's houses and tenements, chapels, fish cellars and seasonal residences including the Tower. Business man, J.T. Treffry, of Place Manor in Fowey, became the new owner and carried on the expansion that eventually lead to Newquay becoming a holiday resort!

The pictures included here show some of the people, the type of lives they led and the stages of change and development in the town which created the foundations of the Newquay we know today.

Joyce Greenham, Bard Lowena Lywans, and Sheila Harper
Newquay, May 1999

An early view of Newquay Harbour. This is before 1872 when a jetty was added to the harbour. In the foreground is a wooden gantry. Fish were unloaded from boats straight onto it and into the Active Fish Cellar. On the left in the distance is Towan Beach and behind it Speculation Fish Cellar. It is backed by a much larger edifice the use of which can only be guessed at. Further along are the buildings where Treffry's Cellar was once situated, but the overall shape bears little resemblance to later structures here. Further right is an indistinct white building. This is said to be the Salt House where salt was stored for preserving fish.

Acknowledgements

Newquay's image is one of a post-Victorian seaside resort that sprung up out of nothing. We, with the help of our own archives and that of the Newquay Old Cornwall Society (NOCS), hope to show you that this town has a rich heritage. The work included here is part of ongoing research about our area and there is still much to be done. Some of the information given is anecdotal or from notes written on the back of old photographs, so we beg forgiveness if we have made errors. You, the reader, we hope will contact us and correct these. All the information we have brought together, new and old, is a valuable contribution to our local history. We hope this archive book will stimulate others to provide more information about our area to enrich the NOCS Archive. Already many Newquay people, both past and present, have helped us, sometimes unwittingly, to compile this work and we would like to offer our sincere thanks to you all; and humblest apologies to those that we have omitted.

Mrs Poppy Rundle, Mrs Joan Malone, Mr P. Murrin, Pip Staffieri, Reg Morris, Neil Pedlar, Courtney Smale, Roger Jenkin, Roger Lacy, Peter Hicks, O.J. Padel, T. Stephens, S.J. Hebdige, Newquay Old Cornwall Society Archive – especially the work of Miss R.P. Hirst, Messrs. E.J. Ennor and G. White. Woolf-Greenham Photographic Collection, Foxall-Hebdige Postcard Collection, *Ships of North Cornwall* by John Bartlett, *Road Vehicles* by Fisher Barnham, *Old Newquay* by S. Teague Husband, *Newquay – the Story of a Cornish Town* by David Woolgrove and Michael Haigh, and Newquay Old Cornwall Society Publications: *Seafaring* by E.J. Ennor, *Local Shipbuilding* by E.J. Ennor, *NOCS Fifty Years of Events, Personalities and Records* edited by Charles Woolf, *The Start of Newquay* by Rod Lyon (Federation of Old Cornwall Societies), *Looking Back, Newquay part 1* by S.C. May, *Around Newquay* by Bob Acton, *Newquay's Pictorial Past* by Newquay Old Cornwall Society and published by Bob Acton, *Newquay Town Trail Walkabout* by Cornwall Heritage Project, Cornwall County Planning Department, *A Newquay Cottage or Local Pioneers of Education in Newquay* by Roger Jenkin, *The Story of Glendorgal* by Nigel Tangye, *Wrecks Around the Cornish Coast* by Richard Gillis, Newquay Old Cornwall Society archival material – unpublished: *The Homeland Hand Book of Newquay, c. 1909.*

One

The Growth of Newquay and Its Harbour

The eighteenth century was a boom time for the little village of Newquay, its surrounds and the harbour. By 1800, thirteen fish cellars were in operation in the area. Methodist meetings were being held in 'New Key' and travelling preacher William Bryan encouraged local 'Bryanites' to build the first meeting house. This was constructed on land on Towyn Common in 1810 and its site is now the Salvation Army Hall at the bottom of Crantock Street. New roads were being cut. There was an annual regatta in the bay and ship building at Tregunnel, on the River Gannel. Lomax expanded the south pier in the harbour. A few more visitors were coming for the sea air. The Red Lion Inn and large houses, like the Tower and the Fort, were being built for visitors to spend the season here, some taking up permanent residence. Between 1831 and 1841 the population doubled to 488. The first postmistress was appointed. Then Joseph Thomas Treffry firmly set the ball of prosperity rolling. He built the north arm of the harbour and connected the south pier to his china clay pit at Hendra by a horse-drawn railway, the tramtrack. Newquay was born.

Newquay, *c.* 1880. At this time the population was 1,800. Marcus Hill is seen as a farm track, formerly called Trenance Lane. Fish cellars are visible around the harbour. There is no Atlantic Hotel yet on the Headland. Eothen, built for Richard Tredwen, a Padstow shipwright, around 1855, stands alone to the left of the harbour, its veranda clearly visible. Behind it are the long gardens and cottages belonging to the coastguard. Prout's Hotel, now the Red Lion, one of five inns at the time, stands above the harbour and behind it Beacon Road extends upwards. The farm building on the left-hand corner of Marcus Hill awaits demolition with Manor Hotel to be built in its place. Francis Hawkey rented this farmland from William Michell of the Fort. Most of the little cottages opposite the end of the road still exist and are now shops, including Tic Toc, a surf shop and the Yorkshire Building Society.

St Michael's Chapel of Ease opened in 1858. By 1873 it had a north aisle and a steeple. On the left in the distance can be seen Watergate Bay cliffs and Porth Island. On the right are houses in Bank Street and East Street. Behind these the top half of a circular shadow is visible, cast by the bridge over the tram track, by the side of Newquay's main post office.

Newquay, from Dane Hill, *c.* 1890. On the skyline are the miners' cottages on Mount Wise. Speculation and Treffry Cellars are at the back of Towan Beach. In 1892 Speculation was 'washed down'. The junction between Tower Road, Fore Street and Beacon Road can be seen, along with the back of Prout's Hotel and the manicured garden of the Fort, residence of Colonel Michell who died in 1892. The formation of the Local Board in 1868 was mainly his doing.

Looking over Newquay Harbour, 1860s. There are ore trucks below to the right and in the wall behind these are chutes. The least indistinct buildings from the left are the long and low Rose Cellar, demolished in 1886, and next to it Colonel Michell's house, the Fort, built in 1830. This had a flagstaff in the grounds, erected in 1870.

The Spider, c. 1870. This shows Tolcarne Viaduct built for Treffry in 1849, the year before he died. Also known as the Tolcarne Spider, spanning Trenance Valley, it was for horse-drawn wagons. It had seventeen pillars, topped with wooden trestles carrying the track at a height of ninety feet above the centre of the valley. Some of the original stonework can still be seen. It linked a tramway from Hendra Clay Pit, St Dennis, with a line from East Wheal Rose Mine, St Newlyn East, to Newquay Harbour.

The harbour jetty was erected, *c.* 1872, by the Cornwall Minerals Railway Co. to increase the working capacity of the harbour, in anticipation of a huge increase in traffic in iron ore, china clay and china stone. It connected with Treffry's horse-drawn mineral tramway, the 'tramtrack', which ended on the harbour via an eighty yard long tunnel. On the left are the rails of the tramtrack running into the tunnel. Just past this is the old Seaman's Mission.

The harbour incline was built for Treffry. By using a winding engine and thick wire cable, trucks on the rails could be pulled up or down the steep slope. Here the trucks are loaded with Welsh coal and timber, brought in by schooner. At the top of the incline the trucks were hitched up to horses, and pulled to the railway station along the tramtrack. This ran from the harbour, along Manor Road and then behind the houses in East Street to cross the road to the railway station opposite.

The stationary winding engine was situated on the Whim, now the site of a supermarket in Fore Street. One engine did the winding and the other could provide spares. Steam driven, one of these had the boiler from Engine No. 3041, *The Queen*. This hauled the Royal Train at Windsor for the Diamond Jubilee of Queen Victoria. The tunnel now houses Newquay gigs at its bottom end.

Horse-drawn trucks being taken from the harbour to Newquay railway station, to pick up china clay, *c*. 1890. The driver has stopped the horses, just as they pass East Pump, now Fat Willy's, at the junction of East Street and the tramtrack. The Local Board sunk the pump around 1876, on the site bought from George Hocking for £2. The pump was up a step from the road and the upstairs was reached through a separate door.

Loading china clay at the harbour. Clay from the truck is shovelled down a chute into the hold of the boat. The last vessel to bring coal to Newquay and take a cargo of china clay out of the harbour did so in 1921. The export of clay out of Newquay was already in decline before the First World War.

Trenance Viaduct, formerly known as Tolcarne Viaduct, showing alterations made in 1874 by the Cornwall Minerals Railway Company, formed by London speculator William Richardson Roebuck. The viaduct had to be strengthened to take steam locomotives whose journey ended at Newquay railway station. From there the trucks were still pulled to above the harbour by horses.

Newquay Harbour. In 1877 the Great Western Railway took over the harbour. Their more efficient way of working doubled the handling of china clay and china stone out of the harbour to 4% of the total production from the St Austell area. Here we see a busy and prosperous little harbour.

Shipbuilding yards in Newquay were to be found at Tregunnel on the Gannel, Island Cove at Towan Beach, Porth and here at the harbour. The Quay Yard (centre) was started in 1849 by John and Martyn Clemens. They built nine vessels here, including the schooners *Treffry*, *Tower*, and *Kate*. Richard Tredwen, of Eothen, had the yard for a time and he built at least two vessels. Around 1861, Martyn Clemens came back and built the *Kitty* and *Forest Deer*. Later a general shipwright's business was carried on at the yard by T. and J. Clemens, sons of John. There was always work to be done on boats using the harbour. Thomas' sons, Albert and Richard worked there until 1897. Their father died in 1906 and so ended a long Clemens family association with Quay Yard. Today there is a café on the site.

The Fairy Maid coming through the gap. A fine schooner built in the Gannel Yard in 1877 by T. and J. Clemens, her managing owners were W.B. Williams and then W.H. Williams. Her masters were J. Williams, J. Reeler and E. Cleness. Sailing from Runcorn for Newquay with coal, she was stranded and then wrecked near Holyhead on 20 December 1919; the crew were saved. On 8 January 1920 her crew were rescued from the same spot. Perhaps they had returned to try to salvage the cargo.

Captain Joseph Albert Hicks died at Belmont Place at the ripe old age of ninety-five in 1905. Here he takes a couple of rays home for his tea. He was master of a number of vessels including the *Johnson and Elizabeth*, named after his parents, and the *Victoria*.

The Hind in Newquay Harbour. She was built in Cardiff in 1862. She has a small figurehead of a young deer painted white. Nicholas House of Newquay bought her in 1889 and R. Hockin, A. Andrews and W. Cock were her masters. W. Cock was her master when she was wrecked off Ireland in a force 10 gale in 1905. All four crew members were saved.

The Vixen was built at the Island Cove Yard by J. Osborne. Here she is sailing in to the harbour with a hobbler's boat in attendance, *c.* 1900. She had a long career, being lengthened at the Gannel Yard around 1873 when E.L. Johns of Crantock took her over from E.A. Martyn and J. Osborne, her first owners. After ten years she went to a Lerryn owner, then in 1912 G. Irons of Newquay had an interest in her. She had another owner and was taken off register in 1923, after being broken up.

William Henry, R.H.G., and *The Camellia* in harbour before 1887. The *William Henry* was built at Feock in 1854. Sometime in the 1880s James Trebilcock acquired her. Thomas Jacka took her over in 1897. Both were Newquay men. By 1904 she was back with a Truro owner. *R.H.G.* was named after her builder, R.H. Gilbert. From 1881 she traded out of Newquay, captained by Robert Hooper Hoyle, with his sons, James aged eighteen and William aged thirteen, as his crew. Captain Galsworthy then took her over with his son as crew. The story goes that on coming back from Spain, the captain brought her through the 'gap' into harbour single handed, as his son was sleeping and he did not want to wake him! A great feat at any time. *The Camellia* was John Ennor's, with W. Trebilcock as her Newquay master. Henwood took over and was captain when she collided with the SS *Moss Rose* in 1897 and sunk off the Lizard. No lives were lost.

Pleasure steamers brought day trippers from as far away as Ilfracombe to spend the day in Newquay. *Johann Carl, Hetty, Fairy Maid* and *Katie* are in harbour in 1912. On the right is the steamer.

The paddle steamers, including probably the *Brighton*, featured here *c.* 1906, were operated out of Bristol and proved very popular taking visitors on trips from Ilfracombe, Barry and Mumbles and other such places. Several times a season they would make for Padstow and occasionally Newquay. However, when the tide was out there was no water in Newquay Harbour. This meant that the only way the excursionists could get into town was by being disembarked and landed using small craft. This provided good entertainment for local people, watching wobbly-legged visitors trying to get into the rowing boats, missing and falling into the water.

Two

Fishing

Pilchard fishing was seasonal and involved the whole community. Its history goes back a long way. The Survey of Cornwall, written by Carew, in the reign of Elizabeth I, describes pilchard fishing as the third biggest industry of the time. Pilchards, large sardines, eat plankton which they follow around the ocean. At times they swim near the coast into the bays, sometimes in vast numbers, where they could be caught by 'seining'. This involved encircling the shoal with a seine net. The net was then hauled into shallow water from the shore via a rope attached to it. Next a smaller tuck net was used to gather together some of the fish inside the big net. These pilchards were then lifted out of the water into a tuck boat using a wicker basket.

The huers, c. 1863. From left to right, S. Clemens, Captain C. Carter and Jim Clemens lean against the fourteenth-century Huer's Hut, on Towan Headland. Messrs Carter and Clemens hold long zinc plated tin 'horns', megaphones through which they would shout 'Hevva, Hevva' to alert the fishermen on the sea, and all the villagers for that matter, that pilchards were sighted in the bay. There were a number of fishing companies in Newquay, called 'seines', each with a fish cellar, men, boats and all the equipment used to catch and process the pilchards. When a shoal was present each seine worked a stated section of the bay. It was the huer's job to direct their seine towards the fish by waving signalling devices.

Seine boats in the harbour, oars stowed ready to be off, nets carefully and neatly folded to be shot at speed.

Pilchards ready for unloading. The baskets, used for getting the pilchards out of the tuck net into the boat, were called flaskets. They were designed to drain quickly. *The John*, behind the pilchard boats, was owned by Alex Stephens of Porth from 1893. She foundered after leaving Mumbles in November 1900.

From left to right Active, Good Intent, and Fly Cellars, in the 1890s. Fly and Good Intent burnt down in 1922. Fly is now a promenade. One of the largest cellars was the Active above the north pier of the harbour. The council took it over in 1905, and what is left of the buildings has become a public amenity. Cellars were above ground, generally with a loft and constructed around a courtyard.

Fly Cellar is said to have been built in 1800. The pilchards were taken to the cellars where women bulked the fish. This meant putting them in layers with salt, under cover below the fish loft. The pile could be five feet high and some feet thick and stretch all around the covered part of the cellar. The men from left to right are Rube Trethewey, Dick Gustave, W. Paul and Benno Bennetto. When the pilchards were gone Fly was used as a herring curing factory.

Active Cellar had ceased use before 1896. The old man on the left is sitting on a gurry, a wheelless barrow used to carry nets and fish across sand and uneven surfaces. The bulked pilchards stood for some weeks in their piles. Their weight on each other caused oil and salty juices to drain from them into a gully, leading to a pit where the liquid could be collected. The men would add more salt to the outside of the pile of fish as required.

Unity Cellar was on the upper promenade down Beach Road just past the Old Malthouse. It was built around 1800 and its contents sold off in 1896. Here it is in a state of disrepair, but imagine those 'bulks' of pilchards in the shadows, now ready to be broken apart. A flat, spade-like implement was carefully used to remove a number of fish. These were shaken in 'wriggles' to remove as much salt as possible. Next the fish were washed, rinsed and packed into barrels by the women.

Outside Active Cellar. In the penthouse, a sheltered area on the side of a cellar, men sit chatting. In earlier days, instead there would have been a row of nearly straight-sided barrels, slightly leaky, ready for women to neatly pack the fish in. A loose lid was put on each barrel and the fish were pressed down by means of a suspended weight pushing on it. More oil came out and ran in to the pit. More fish were added as the contents were compressed. Barrels took about a week to fill. They were then sealed and made ready for export.

Unity Cellar china. At the end of the pilchard-fishing season everyone deserved a treat after all their hard work. A troil would be held in the loft above the cellars. This included a feast (hence the lovely china), dancing and games, and could last well into the night. One of the last troils to be held in Newquay was at the Rose Cellars in 1883.

Pipe smoking Cad Carter, Eli Clemens and Joker Pearce pose in a studio for this shot. Wallace Bennetto was a professional photographer, so this could have been one of his pictures. Some of the outdoor harbour and cellar scenes were taken by Fairfax Ivimey. A wealthy man, he acquired the Fort after the death of Colonel Michell and took a keen interest in local history. It was he who took the anchor, found at sea by John Clemens, from Quay Yard and placed it in the Fort grounds.

Boiling up seal oil at Active Cellar, c. 1901. Fairfax Ivimey took this picture. We know this because Peter Hick's great-grandfather just missed being in the scene. The men are from left to right, Stanley Mitchell cutting up the blubber, Sam Clemens stoking the fire, Joe Hicks with the coal, 'Piper' (William) Matthews with his dog and Captain Edwin Clemens holding up the seal skin. Seal oil extracted from the blubber was used to treat rheumatism and arthritis.

Red fish and blue fish were another source of income for the men of Newquay. Edible crabs are the red fish and lobsters the blue. Crayfish and spider crabs were also caught. The pots were made from withies, still being cut as late as 1958, from the osier beds at Rialton, St Columb Minor. Other sources were at Treago, near Crantock and behind Trevarrian near Watergate Bay. Payment was in kind, perhaps a couple of rabbits or crayfish left on a doorstep or a parcel of fish sent via the local bus.

The Mackerel Fleet in Newquay Harbour at the turn of the century. Inshore pilchard fishing was no longer viable. Only one seine was still working in Newquay in 1907. There was a brief period of local herring fishing in the 1900s, but it was only for a few months a year and hard to make a living out of.

The Porthleven fleet leaving harbour. Porthleven had a large herring fishing fleet and its boats, which used Newquay, would have had a PZ for Penzance registration. They sometimes fished with the Newquay fleet. The attraction Newquay held for herring fisheries was that it had a railway so the fish could be transferred quickly to their destination.

Off-loading the herrings. The fish were carried to shore and put in barrels with salt. Behind the herring boats, the *Amanda* can be made out. She had a long career. She was built at Padstow in 1867 for Captain Henry House and was still sailing in the 1930s, when she was abandoned at Pont Pill, Fowey.

Herring fishing was undertaken using a drift net, here being shaken out. It must be an interesting sensation being knee-deep in fish. Perhaps 300,000 herrings would be landed at a time.

Net mending, here taking place below the Active Cellar, required a lot of patience. This was performed using a shuttle and a knotting technique. The nets also had to be treated with preservative to stop them rotting. This was achieved by soaking them in the brown tannin rich liquid acquired from steeping oak bark in water.

Buyers in attendance, no doubt checking the quality of the herrings, before the filled barrels are hauled up the incline in trucks and from there taken to the railway station. The fish fetched about 1d each. Sometimes if there was a big catch three or four trains a day would be needed to get the fish to London in the best condition.

Three

Newquay's Lifeboats and Life-savers

True courage is to risk one's life to save another's. What does it take to enter a dangerous sea on a quest to rescue persons unknown? Only the lifeboat men know and if you pose the question they'll just shrug their shoulders and maybe grin. Newquay has its share of these heroes. The wooden rowing boats of yesteryear have long been superseded by fast diesel-powered inflatable inshore vessels but they and the men who manned them are not forgotten.

The *Willie Rogers* was in service from 1892 until 1899. She was self righting, thirty-four feet long and had ten oars. Here she is coming through the gap into Newquay Harbour. The men wear woolly hats and cork life jackets. Like all Newquay's lifeboats from the first, the *Joshua* in service from 1861, she had to be launched from a beach, pulled there on her carriage by horses, from the lifeboat house in Fore Street. In 1895 the *Escurial* was in distress off Newquay in dreadful heavy seas. Three attempts were made to launch the *Willie Rogers* without success. The *Escurial* went on to drift ashore at Portreath. St Ives and Hayle lifeboats were also unsuccessful in reaching the ship. The outcome of all this was the construction of one of the 'steepest slipways in Britain' into deep water at Towan Head, Newquay.

The Rocket Apparatus, crew, and members of the coastguard after 1900. In 1843, nine Dennets Rockets were placed at Newquay. These could be used to fire ropes from the shore to ailing vessels. This type of equipment was still in use at the turn of the century and has saved many lives. The apparatus was eventually kept in the Rocket House, which still exists in Hope Terrace, surrounded by iron railings, and is a motor repair shop at present.

Rocket practice, probably above Lusty Glaze Beach.

Newquay Lifeboat Day, *c.* 1900. In the afternoon a large crowd gathered to watch the launch of the lifeboat from the Headland slipway and its eventual arrival at Towan Beach, where it was put back on its horse-drawn carriage and hauled up to the lifeboat house.

Royal visit in 1909, with the lifeboat team and horses, loaned by Mr Alex Stephens (wearing the boater), awaiting inspection by the Prince and Princess of Wales. From left to right: Mr Stanley Flamank's father, Mr Alex Stephens who supplied the horses (he lived at Porth Veor and was a merchant, owning the coal yards at Porth, he was also a ship owner), -?-, Mr Bray, Mr Hawke of Mawgan Porth, Mr Hawke's brother, Mr Hawkey and Mr Pascoe.

James Stevens No. 5 and crew, at the lifeboat house on the Headland for the Prince of Wales' visit, *c.* 1909. In December 1917 the *Osten* was in trouble off Newquay in a terrible gale. The new coxswain had declined to go to sea in such weather but former cox Gill said he had been out in worse. R. Trebilcock, J. Clemens, R. and F. Pearce, R. Woodward, J. Grigg, R. Trethewey, J. Hicks, S. Hoar and Captains Hicks and Pappin volunteered to go with Gill. The lifeboat was launched and set sail to the cheers of onlookers. Then a great wave tipped her up, her sails filled with water and she could not self right. Gill and Pappin were washed overboard and managed to make land. The boat drifted into the cliffs and everyone was rescued. Some of the crew had hypothermia and Clemens was badly hurt. Despite not reaching the *Osten*, which survived, Gill and Trebilcock were awarded RNLI gallantry medals which they justly deserved. Too badly damaged, the *James Stevens No. 5* finished its career.

James Stevens No. 5 and crew, 1911, being inspected by Prince Edward and Prince Albert, who became George VI.

Reverend H.C. Muller, seated on the right next to John Bellingham, was chaplain to the Newquay Lifeboat. It is possible these men are a Lifeboat Committee. From left to right, back row are: Whor Stephens, William Pascoe, -?-, Mr Horler Senior, Ned Burt (who 'blasted the sewer'), and Tal Osborne.

Last of the lifeboats. In 1936, the *Admiral Sir George Back*, in service for fourteen years, was sold for £60, sadly ending, as far as local people were concerned at the time, Newquay's association with lifeboats forever. February, and the day of removal to Poole in Dorset, came. The boat had been slung to the beams of the boat house so that a lorry and tender could be run underneath. One of the blocks supporting the boat broke and it took several more days to shift her. The *Admiral* didn't want to go! Josephus Harris was her last coxswain.

THE GREAT BLIZZARD of March 10th, 1891.

FOUR NEWQUAY VESSELS LOST.

One full crew only saved (Capt R. J. HOCKIN and five men).

NEWQUAY VESSELS LOST :—

"FAIRY BELLE," Captain LEWIS, with all hands.

"AGNES LOUISA," Captain HAM, with all hands.

"PORTH," Captain J. BILLING, who, with his son, remained on board, were saved ; but C. BOXER, mate, a well-known Newquay swimmer, swam to one of the Scilly Islands, and was later found frozen to death.

"ETHEL," Captain R. J. HOCKIN, and five men were all saved.

The " Fairy Belle " and " Agnes Louisa " foundered, and the " Porth " and " Ethel " became total wrecks. The " Ethel's " boat (which brought the Crew ashore) is now being exhibited.

NEWQUAY has vivid and sad memories of the great blizzard which swept the United Kingdom for three days and caused the loss of a large number of ships all round the coast. Four coasting vessels of Newquay were among the number. Two went down with all hands. The fourth was the " Ethel," commanded by Newquay's present Harbour Master (Captain R. J. Hockin), which struck on the rocks of the North Devon Coast and became a total wreck on the 10th March, 1891, when the gale was at its height. By great efforts the crew reached land safely in the small boat. This gallant little craft is now being exhibited on Mr. HEDLEY WESTLAKE's premises (by kind permission of the Council and Captain Hockin), as an example of what can be done by a tiny cockleshell when properly handled.

Launched by hand from the doomed ship, fast breaking up on the rocks at the foot of the high cliffs, up which it was impossible to scale, the little boat started on her memorable voyage, while the gale was still at its greatest height. Scudding dead before it, she ran grave risk of being swamped by the heavy seas which threatened at any moment to overwhelm her. Two of the crew sat on the stern so as to form a breakwater, and on their backs the seas broke again and again, thus preventing the seas from filling and swamping the boat, which would have otherwise happened. Two others tended an oar each to help to keep her from broaching to, while the fifth baled continuously with a bucket which had been placed in her by wise forethought of the Captain. Handled with superb seamanship, the sturdy little boat brought her crew safely to land at Combe Martin, 13 miles from the scene of the wreck, in blinding snow and intense cold. The boat is worthy of a close study, for there is probably not another one in the Kingdom with such a record. On landing, the half-frozen men were cared for by the Hon. Agent of the Shipwrecked Mariners' Society, and as soon as possible sent to their homes in Newquay, where they learned the sad news of the loss of so many of their friends and fellow seamen.

Captain HOCKIN has kindly lent his boat for Exhibition in aid of the funds of The Shipwrecked Mariners' Society, in the hope that many will be moved, by the story of her gallant struggle against fearful odds, to assist the Society to provide for shipwrecked men of to-day as it did for the crew she brought ashore.

WILLIAMS, PRINTERS, NEWQUAY.

A description of the Great Blizzard.

Four

From Central Square to Narrowcliff

In the seventeenth century the hamlet of Towan Blystry was gathered around what is now known as Central Square. From there was a track leading to the harbour called Quay Road, which went on to the Huer's House on the headland. Tracks also led to Crantock and Towan Beach and the fields behind it. There were a number of farms in the area and, way along the coast, St Columb Porth, which gave the parish its name. By 1837 the little village, now Newquay, had eighty-six houses. In 1851 there was one shop, owned by Robert Sleeman which sold groceries and simple medicines. What a contrast with today!

Commercial Square, c. 1900. The biggest building in the square, which is more of triangle, was the Commercial Hotel. There was an inn on the site in 1755, which by 1837, in a lease granted to Wm. Parkyn, was known as the Old Inn. He ran a cobbler's shop over the arch and his wife served the drinks. The lease expired, the inn was demolished and the Commercial Hotel erected in 1859. John Ennor had the contract for carpentry and joinery work, which was worth £239 plus £13 10s for 'painting in a plain colour'. It was renamed the Central by 1915. This picture also shows the town water force pump, which replaced an earlier windlass and kibble! It was used for supplying the schooners with fresh water and in 1871 each vessel had to pay '6d per voyage'. By 1873 this was increased to 1s, the Local Board getting 3d. They needed the money as the pump often suffered with all the comings and goings of vehicles. In 1873 it was much injured and the Board held an inquiry. In 1882 the handle was removed because the water was thought to have been the cause of a typhoid outbreak.

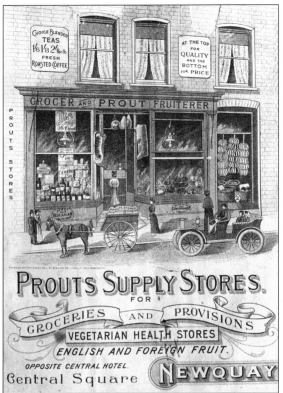

Prout's supply stores, c. 1915. There is nothing new in the world. This advertisement for Prout's also catered for vegetarians, though how they managed to pass under the sides of bacon hanging over the portal without flinching, one cannot say. They had a store at Porth as well. Prout's was opposite the Central Hotel, along with Henry Martyn, ironmonger and builders merchant. T. Jewel, saddler was next door.

The Commercial Hotel, c. 1900, and the 'bus' used to taxi people to and from the railway station. It was owned by A. Hoyte, GWR Agent, who had his agency in 1895.

The Capitol and Counties Bank, c. 1915. This is now Lloyd's Bank, designed by Sylvanus Trevail. In 1957, when it was Barclay's, during excavation at the back of the building to provide extra rooms, about fifteen feet down, a mine adit was discovered appearing to run in an easterly direction. This would likely have been part of the Newquay Silver and Lead Mine, based at Lehenvor, nowadays Mount Wise, where the old Water Board buildings still are. Next door to the bank, now an arcade, is the Central Motor Co. In each of the rear corners of the garage, there was a slate slab covering a spring.

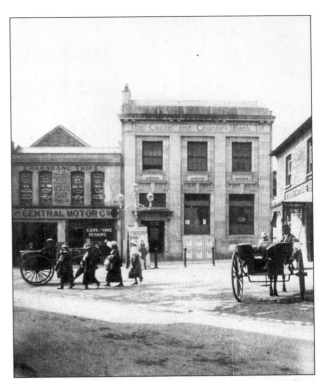

Matthews Dairy and Café, 1 and 2 Central Square was started by Miss Louie Matthews. Even in the 1950s the dairy retained its charm. There was still the marble counter on top of which was a cloth covered bowl of cream with a good crust, a round of cheese, fresh eggs and bottles of milk. Other foods were sold as well. The café, next door, provided morning coffee, lunches and afternoon tea, hot pasties and meat pies and in summer, fresh strawberry tarts with Cornish cream.

Miss Louie Matthews, founder of Matthews Dairy and Café. She bought the properties from Mr Cardell. She was helped in the dairy by her niece, Miss Ethell Farley and the café was run by her nephew, Reg Matthews and his wife Ivy.

Matthews Dairy, c. 1959 Left to right: Reg Matthews, Miss Ethell Farley and Alice 'Dolly' Matthews.

The India and China Tea Company, at 5 Bank Street, just off Central Square, *c.* 1900. The staff of this tea and provisions shop are all wearing sacking aprons. Is that the delivery boy on the left? One of the group is rather young! Shops with odd door numbers are on the same side of the road as National Westminster Bank and Boots.

The post office was Newquay's first purpose built premises, opened in 1911 and closed in 1970. It was opposite today's Newquay Arms with its the ornate lamp hung over the door. To the right of the building are stone pillars either side of the gates through which the post office delivery vans came and went. Beyond the gates is 'Hawke and Thomas'. Part of the site is now the National Westminster Bank.

Marine Villa, c. 1900. Captain Thomas is standing in the doorway. For over thirty years he kept two tame seagulls, one of which was blind, in the front garden. Looking out of the upstairs window is his son P.H. Thomas. He was at one time the secretary of the local Lifeboat Committee. The post office, built in 1911, was in front of and incorporated into the house.

Hawke and Co., c. 1900. The business at 15 Bank Street, was founded by Mary, Charlotte and Ellen Hawke in 1871. The shop's bank account was held at Messrs. Willyams, Willyams and Co., St Columb. The ladies looked after their young nephew, George Hawke Thomas, from about 1880. After training at Penzance, he joined the business in 1898. He gained further experience in Birmingham and was made a business partner by his aunts in 1905, when the shop changed its name to Hawke and Thomas.

Hawke and Thomas, c. 1909. By this time they had revamped their premises. These now included 'Drapery Goods, Milliner on Premises, Mourning Orders promptly executed'. Note the wonderful bathing suits hanging outside the shop. Hawke Thomas slowly took over the business completely as his aunts died and in 1911 Miss E.L. Libby joined the firm. She eventually became a partner. The shop expanded and moved to 31 Bank Street.

Hawken General Draper and Co. London House. The premises occupied 10, 12 and 14 Bank Street, on the Newquay Arms side of the road. This large shop sold everything from collars to carpets. Nos 12 and 14 at present are occupied by Oliver's shoe shop.

Osborne's tobacconist and confectioners. This is 14 Bank Street, originally Hawken's, with the owner standing proudly in her doorway. Note the Rex Toffee vending machine on the left.

J. Westlakes. This very old picture shows Westlakes, 18 to 22 Bank Street, saddler and ironmonger. The couple standing in the door are almost certainly Mr and Mrs Westlake. In 1919 the shop was reduced in size and eventually bought by Mr Palmer who slowly replaced the shop goods with quality toys and leather goods. The name Westlake was retained until Mr Palmer closed the shop in 1971. It now sells ladies fashion ware.

Bank Street, c. 1909. Looking towards Central Square. Lloyd's Bank, on the corner of Beachfield Avenue, opened in 1906. It was designed by Sylvanus Trevail for the Devon and Cornwall Banking Co. and was occupied in 1910 by Madame Hawke for the manufacture and display of knitwear. There was a substantial knitted goods industry in Newquay. It is now a shoe shop. Opposite is Commercial House and Pardy's. Pardy's Boarding House, Restaurant and Temperance Hotel was run by Mr and Mrs W.J. Pardy. In the road is the Town Porter's wagon making a delivery.

T.A. Hubber, fruiterer and greengrocers. Emma Hubber stands in front of the shop at 19 Bank Street. Her husband, Thomas, had a pony and trap for hire and used to take the Prince of Wales to the golf club when he was in town. The shop was later moved to 7A Bank Street, now part of Threshers. Hubbers, the florist in Central Square, opened in 1946.

Hartnoll's, *c*. 1911. It closed in 1946. Lloyd's Bank can be seen in the distance, then Huxtables which became part of Redruth Brewery, next Giles and Henwood at No. 39. E. Giles and Son Tailors still operates from here today. Hartnoll's was a stationers, printers, lending library, newsagents, bookseller and, like many shops today, retailed all manner of other goods. It was like walking into an Aladdin's Cave stuffed with merchandise from floor to ceiling.

T.H. Clemens, *c*. 1935. When Charles Woolf came to Newquay in 1935 as manager of Boots the Chemist, he remembers that Mr Clemens, pictured, charged 4d for a haircut!

Alfred Bond, chemist, stands in his doorway. He bought the premises from Miss Wallis and opened here, at 45 Bank Street, in 1894. He died in 1947 at his home, Alfra House in Eliot Gardens. He was a Founder Trustee of the Wesley Methodist church in East Street and a district and county councillor. His second wife, Miss Trelease, assisted Mr Bond in his shop. Before 1909 he was making Bonds Neroline Lotion: 'For removing Sunburn, Redness, Roughness, Freckles, Tan and other Blemishes, and making the Skin and Complexion delightfully clear and Soft. Delicately Perfumed. In Bottles, One Shilling Each'.

Chymedden, the home of Dr Hickey. This imposing house, opposite the corner of Bank Street and Manor Road has now been replaced by flats. In the front garden is Barclay's Bank. On the left is H.G. Slee and Co. In the late 1920s it was the tourist information bureau and was run by Harry Sanderson, today it is Hunters.

East Street, *c.* 1912. Looking towards Bank Street, in the centre distance the tram track passing into Manor Road can be seen. On the left of that is a very tiny building which was the Falmouth Steam Laundry Office. The first shop on the left is Oxenberry and Sons, grocer at 28 East Street, which was founded by W. Oxenberry in Oakleigh Terrace in 1906, and moved to East Street two years later. Past a couple of houses is E. Powell's cycle shop. In February 1950 Oxenbury's and W.J.B. Knight of Berry Road went into partnership.

H. Garlick and Son, 19 November 1909. The first building on the seaward side of the road backing onto the tram track was the triangular shaped Pump House, where water could be obtained. The next shop along was Garlick's, who also had 3 Cheltenham Place. The odd-shaped pavement is still there today.

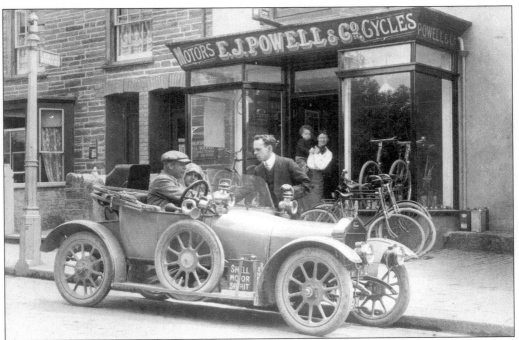

E.J. Powell and Co., *c.* 1912. This was situated at 8 East Street. Mr Jenkin, in the car, is shaking the hand of Mr Powell; his wife and child are in the background. Powell also hired out perambulators, trolley cars and was sole agent for 'His Master's Voice Gramophones'. Next door was W. Furse, sail and bathing tent maker.

Woodward's Garage, *c.* 1918. Now the site of Argos, Woodwards were the pioneers of charabanc tours in Newquay. By 1920 they were offering sixteen different tours in the summer, four of which went into Devon. As the town got busier, they used to have problems trying to get vehicles in and out of the garage.

Victoria Parade, East Street was a terrace of imposing houses built in 1898 by Bellingham, which still exist today as shops including John Nance, furnishers. At 52 East Street, Thomas Walker's 'The Newquay Art Gallery', in 1911, boasted the largest gallery in Cornwall, and was still there in 1926.

Dorothy Café, Victoria Parade in 1900, when it was owned by Evans Brown. It was still Dorothy's in the 1970s. Sam Malone was baker here. It later became Ellery's Bakery and in 1980 the original oven was still in situ.

Hotel Victoria. Newquay. *Date built — 1897.*

No. of Rooms. 100

E. M. Williams

Hotel Victoria. Mr Bray of Forest Hill in Kent collected information about hotels. He sent this card on 6 August 1906, to the Victoria asking for the date built, number of rooms and the autograph of the proprietor on the front of the view. Mr E.M. Williams duly replied and sent the card back the very next day. One of the prestigious hotels built in Newquay at the turn of the century, this one was built by Bellingham.

Hotel Victoria under construction, *c.* 1897. This hotel is unique in having a lift, inside a tunnel, down to Great Western Beach, which is still in working order.

Station Road, *c.* 1907. The row of houses on the right is Victoria Terrace in Station Road (Cliff Road today), leading to Berry Road. All these houses are now shops including Daisy Chain and the Outdoor Camping Leisure Shop. In 1906, nos 1, 3, 4 and 6 were let to visitors by Mrs Bennett, Mrs James, Mrs Radcliffe and Mrs Gill. Next there is a gap where the tram track ran across the road to the railway station. In the distance can be seen the end wall of Forbuoys and Tolcarne Road.

"Beachcroft" Newquay

Beachcroft Hotel, Cliff Road, just past the Griffin, began as two private houses. One was Beaucliffe House, built around 1872, and was lived in by Mr J.V. Sigvald Muller. He was a pupil of Brunel, the famous engineer, and Honorary Chief Consulting Engineer to Great Western Railway. He oversaw the conversion of the North Cornwall Mineral Railway into a passenger line. The other house, Cliff Garth, built around 1896, was for Revd A.H. Molesworth, St Aubyn. In 1927 the houses were joined and extended.

Station Road, *c.* 1906. It is hard to imagine that these houses, between Beachcroft and the Blue Lagoon, with their pretty canopies over the doors and around some of the windows, are now all shops selling everything from jewellery to surf gear.

Great Western Hotel, *c.* 1909. This was built by J.H. Whitfield, solicitor, opposite the railway station. The first owner was also a basket maker and bathing machine proprietor. In 1909 the first of three generations of Hooper's took over. These being J.V., C.V. (Bosun) and Jeremy. When J.V. Hooper took over the hotel it was completely refurbished. He also offered 'Hacks and Hunters' on hire.

Narrowcliff, *c.* 1909. Just past the Great Western Hotel, Newquay finally boasts a promenade above the cliffs, with glorious sea views and yards of seats for the elderly. Narrowcliffe has since changed nearly beyond recognition. Gardens are car parks and these houses have disappeared under alterations and extensions. Locals called this area the 'West End'. A favourite pastime on a Sunday afternoon was to go and watch the fine ladies and gentlemen promenade up and down Narrowcliff.

Tolcarne Hotel, Narrowcliff, is a good example reflecting how Newquay grew in popularity. Here the hotel has had to take on an annexe. The building was extended further and today this view is unrecognisable.

Five
Fore Street and Area

New mansions and villas were built along the lane connecting the harbour with Central Square. In 1835 the Red Lion Hotel was built above the harbour where Tower Road met Quay Road. It was decided to rename the stretch from the square to the inn and so in 1837, Newquay had its first street, Fore Street.

Fore Street and A. Jenkins Stores, *c.* 1910. They sold groceries, provisions, glass and china. One of Newquay's oldest shops, Captain F. Jenkin, sold coal, corn and groceries from around the 1850s. His son and wife extended the business in 1883 adding china, paraffin, treacle and miners dips to the range of goods sold. In 1909 the shoe shop next door was purchased; it is shown selling china. Next was a complete revamping of the store, when the clock tower and bowed glass shop fronts were added, which still exist today. Now the store was known as 'Big Jenks'.

Stephens' Café, No. 6 Fore Street, *c.* 1920. The ladies are Miss Lilian Sleeman and the Misses Irene and Marjory Stephens.

Fore Street, *c.* 1915. Looking towards Central Square, Jenkin's Stores is on the right. On the left is Clifford's, a drapers and milliners and Newquay Dairy Co. On the extreme left is Bert Lambert in front of his shop. He was born in Chelsea and started his career with W.H. Smiths on Paddington Station. He took over Wilshire's Library and Stationers in 1909. A strong man, he won the Sandow Belt for weightlifting.

H.G. Slee, fruitier and florist, at 43 Fore Street, *c*. 1930. On the left is Kathleen Woodward who later had her own florist business. On the right is Miss Slee.

The Sailor's Arms, Fore Street at the turn of the century. The licensee standing outside is Mr F. Daniel. Next door is A. Huxtable's posting establishment, now incorporated in the inn.

N. Grigg, stationer and fancy dealer at Treloy House, Fore Street, nearly opposite the old Lifeboat House, *c.* 1910. Treloy is the name of a farm just outside Newquay, where there is an ancient Holy Well, whose water was purported to cure diseased 'legges'.

Fore Street, looking towards Central Square, *c.* 1915. The Cornwall Laundry Co. Ltd also hired out motor cars, and sold goods to visitors. In the centre of the picture just before the cottages is the old Lifeboat house, already a shop. The cottages were for the coastguards and were eventually demolished to make way for a car park.

The coastguard station and cottages, built in 1825. This was the first terrace built in Newquay and locals remember them as 'the buildings'. When demolished their gardens became West End Bowling Green. The old Lifeboat House at the end of the terrace was built in 1860 to house the first lifeboat, the *Joshua*.

Fore Street, *c.* 1915. On the right are the monumental masons, Evans and Sons which stood in the gardens of Shirley Cottage hidden by shrubbery. Shirley Cottage, housed a school in the kitchen from at least the 1860s. It was run by Jane Sleeman, whose father was Cap'n Bob Sleeman. On the left is the Fort, built in 1830. It was bought by Wm. Michell, barrister and vice warden of the Stannary Courts around 1839, from Humphrey Williams Esq. of Carnanton. Wm. Michell's son, William Edward Michell lived there for the rest of his life. He was one of the men who helped to turn Newquay from a village into a town.

Prout's Hotel was built in 1835 by Mrs Thomas, who took out a ninety-nine year lease on the land. It was originally called the Red Lion. By 1873 Mr Prout took it over and it became known as Prout's Hotel. When he died, around 1882, his wife moved and opened a private hotel further up Fore Street, where Tregurrian House is now. Sampson Stephens took over the building and renamed it The Red Lion once again, and it remains thus today.

The Red Lion, Red Lion Square, decked out for the 1909 visit of the Prince and Princess of Wales. The proprietor then was R. Coumbe. Compare with the picture of Prout's Hotel. It now sports a balcony. The Atlantic Hotel is in the background.

T. Jacka, grocer, corn and coal merchant, and tobacconist had his shop from around 1900 on the corner of Tower and Beacon Road. It was also the Beacon Road post office and Thomas Jacka was the sub-postmaster. He was born at Rose in 1852. He went to America with his brother Samuel for thirteen years where they worked in the gold diggings in California and returned to Newquay in 1888. He was a member of the Newquay Urban District Council and a magistrate.

The Headland Hotel, Little Fistral Meadow, was completed in 1900. Sylvanus Trevail, its architect was also chairman of the Headland Hotel Company that built it. Work started in 1897. At the same time the Atlantic Hotel began to build a wall along Beacon Road from the top of Dane Road to prevent motor cars toppling into the sea. Local people realised that they were losing common rights of access to parts of the headland so they pulled down the wall and railings around the hotel. Then on 31 August 1897 about 100 people, accompanied by a brass band and led by police officers, marched from Commercial Square to Little Fistral Meadow and took apart a wooden office and threw it into the sea. This was the 'Headland Riot'.

The coffee room of the Headland Hotel, October 1911. Every luxury was available, including electric light and a lift.

Atlantic Hotel, War Memorial & Harbour from Island Estate

The Atlantic Hotel on part of the Beacon on Towan Headland dominates the view over town. It opened in 1892 coinciding with an outbreak of scarlet fever in Newquay which put visitors off for a while! Built on behalf of the Cornish Hotels Company, the architect was Sylvanus Trevail.

Sandy Lane, before 1900 when sixteen houses were built and it became Atlantic Road. The Atlantic Hotel, which opened in 1892, can be seen in the distance. The top of Crantock Street is over on the right. Just above centre of the view is a white building, the Tower, with its castellated features. The round part of the tower was built for Captain Frederick Rogers RN around 1835 by John Carne. During the mid-1800s this was the seaside residence of the Gregors of Trewarthenick. When Mr G.W.T. Gregor died the Tower passed to his son-in-law, Sir Paul Molesworth. In 1998, at the end of Atlantic Road (just over the hedge on the left), a settlement dating to around AD 250 was excavated.

Crantock Street, *c.* 1920. Two ladies stand outside the general store, owned by Miss Jenkin. The store was locally nicknamed 'Little Jenks', to distinguish it from 'Big Jenks' in Fore Street. On the left is the, then, new fire station.

Beach Road, leading down to Towan Beach. On the right is the new Pavilion Theatre. On the left up the steps are Beach Cottage and Primrose Cottage, with Primrose House along the path, where Mrs Willey lived in 1895. The Chy-an-Mor Inn is now on this site.

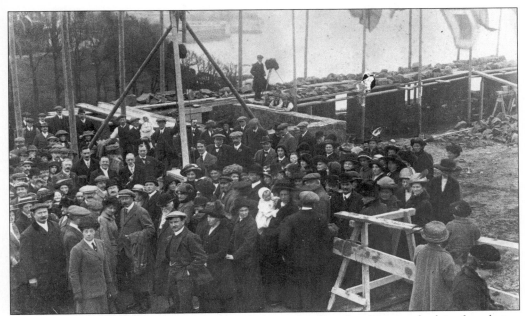

The Pavilion Theatre, by Harbour Crescent, later the Camelot Cinema, had its foundation stone laid in March 1912. Now, in 1999 it is disused, much to local people's dismay. The Pavilion was already part built for Cornish Riviera Entertainments Limited. Mr George Graves of Drury Lane fame laid the stone after a long speech and Mr G.G. Bullmore proposed the vote of thanks. Mr Frederick Dale was the new manager.

The first masonic lodge (on the right), dedicated in 1877, still exists in part, tucked away on land between Beachfield Avenue and Bank Street. It has somehow been incorporated into the shops facing onto Beach Road. The thatched cottage would have been on land between the upper part of Beach Road and Gover Lane.

Going to school, Steps Malthouse, Beach Road. To the right, in his smart sailor suit, is Hugh Muller. Above him are Wally Hawken and John Bellingham (on the right). The Malthouse, where barley was converted to malt for beer making, was demolished in 1922. The building had many uses. It was home to Granny Cook and her husband, a local preacher. Captain R.J. Hockin's father kept a school here from about 1866 to 1870. Dr Hutton also had a school. Mr Furse used it as a sail-making loft. Next Revd J. Trounsell Mugford had his grammar school here then Mr Currah used it for stables. When Union Fish Cellar had to bring in men from Mevagissey and Charlestown to work their seine, these gentlemen slept there. It was used by the Local Board and the under portion by Nankivell and Co. as a wine store. Just past the Malthouse can be seen the side of Unity Fish Cellar.

Six
Entertainment

Entertainment for locals and visitors was richly provided for. Newquay had sports facilities, clubs, societies, charabanc tours and theatres. There were also annual events such as Lifeboat Day and the regatta. People knew how to enjoy themselves.

Lady bicyclists, gather at the bottom of Berry Road, pre-1912. On the right of Knight's the grocers is the post office. W.J.B. Knight and Son was founded around 1893 by Mr Buller Knight, in the then 'new' part of Newquay. Cycling was a very popular activity for everyone and enabled people to travel farther afield than they ever could before by foot. Visitors were encouraged by local holiday guides to bring their 'wheels' and tour out even as far as Tintagel, thirty-two miles away.

Newquay's 'one and all' Football Club. This picture has two dates – 1905/6 or 1909. From left to right the 'Peppermints' are back row: J. North (Oxford House), ? Delbridge, F. Ivimey. Middle row: Sam May, ? Lilburn, Ed Goldsworthy, Stan Carne, Ed Jenkin, Jim Coumbe. Front: Harold Westlake (Hedley Westlake's brother), Piper Matthews, Hubert Ennor, Gorison Chegwidden, A. Harris.

The Football Cup Final, 1 April 1907. All aboard the North Cornwall Coach Company Limited bus, the Newquay team (Peppermints) leave the Red Lion for the game at Wadebridge, wearing red and white favours. A crowd of 3,000 watched Delbridge, May, Jenkin, Dicker, Goldsworthy, Lilburn, Jacka, Chegwidden, Rowe, Harris and Ennor (captain) lose against Torpoint. The score was 4-0. The previous year they had lost 6-1 to the same team. Would they do better in 1908? Note the warning horn being blown, known as a 'yard of tin' it could be made of copper or brass.

Major Trist of Tristford, somewhere in this picture, was one of Newquay's best known early visitors. In 1886 he organised tennis and cricket matches, ladies versus gentlemen. He recorded these and other events at great length in verse. In this picture the men are batting with 'broomsticks'. The ladies won by one run.

Hurling. Major Murray 'throwing up the ball' on Towan Beach. Held in August, two teams played – it might be east versus west Newquay, or married against single, and so on. Up to 400 people could take part. Major Murray was captain of the East Team who wore red ribbons in their buttonholes. The field of play was Newquay's beaches. The ball was a bit smaller than a cricket ball, weighing about 10oz and was covered in silver. Two goals were marked with crosses. The ball was passed from hand to hand and a goal scored by touching the opposition's goal. No goal was allowed for the first 45 minutes. It was a wonderful free-for-all with each side trying to stop the opposition getting the ball or scoring. Charley Farley wears the stetson. The game is still played at St Columb Major and St Ives.

Miss Essington's needlework class. Boaters held in place by large hat pins, the ladies brave the Newquay wind to have their photograph taken. Miss Essington was the daughter of the Revd R.W. Essington of Plen, 2 Tolcarne Head, on the right of the Great Western Hotel. From left to right, standing: -?-, Miss Martyn, Mrs Williams, Miss Essington, Minnie Ham, E. Hocking and Maud Burt. Seated: Miss Barnicoat, Miss Tregaskis, E. Searle, Misses Jennings and Harris. On rugs: Stella Clemens, Edith Harris, Lily Irons, Miss Best, R. Searle.

The Volunteer Rifle Corps, c. 1900. On the back row are Mr Trythall, Hedley Westlake in charge of musketry practice and Dick Mills on the right. The seated men are, from left to right: John Knight, Willie Hawkey, Dr Hardwick Senior (commanding officer), Georgie Master, George Oakley.

Gannel Regatta, 1926. The scene is dominated by the *Ada*, 'pennants flying, dressed overall'. The *Ada*, built in 1876, was acquired eventually by Mr Thomas A. Reid. He had a boat repair yard near where the schooners were built. He brought the *Ada* up the Gannel to prove the river was still navigable. Here she is probably being used as the committee boat from which races were started. Events included boat and pilot gig races, swimming and walking the greasy pole 'liberally slippered'.

The Gannel Regatta, 1922. This included the first gig race, won here by the *Newquay*. The crew from left to right are: Captain Albert Carter (cox), Reg Morris, Tom Bunt, Oswald (Ossie) Hugo, George Pope, Wilfred Jenkin and Claude Trebilcock. This view was taken later in the harbour because the photographer's attempt at a picture of the crew on the Gannel had failed.

Banqueting Hall, Porth, c. 1920. An unlikely venue for concerts was a large cave, just before the bridge over to Porth Island, in the cliff on the right, however it was sadly blown up in 1987. Stars performing there included not just talented local people but the likes of Dame Sybil Thorndyke's mother and Clara Novello. Visitors carried candles for lighting and camping stools to sit on. The cave could seat over 1,000 people and the acoustics must have been wonderful. The last concert was held around 1937.

Amateur theatricals, c. 1916. Newquay's cultural life was greatly enhanced by Mr and Mrs Crosby Smith. He was an ARAM, teaching music locally and at Cathedral Lane, Truro. His wife taught dance and designed theatrical costumes. Both were involved with the local Dramatic and Operatic Society and the Choral and Orchestral Societies. The group are from left to right, back: Gunning Cock, -?-, -?-, Mrs Murray, Mrs Crosby Smith, Mrs Wright, Wallace Bennetto (a local photographer). Seated: Mrs Wilton, -?-. Sitting on the floor: -?-, -?-, Constantine House.

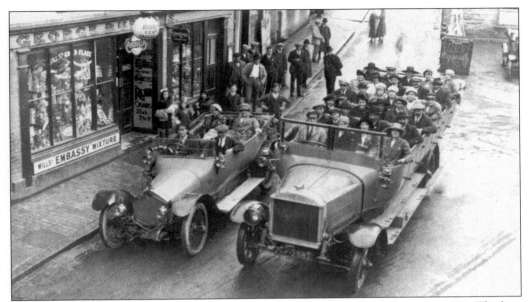

Jenkin's supply stores staff outing to Plymouth, departing from Central Square in 1920. The bus, AF 2582, is a 40 hp Dennis Grey Tourer, from the Newquay Charabanc Company. On the left is an ex-WD 25hp Crossely, AF 2843. Charabanc was originally the name for a horse-drawn vehicle capable of seating at least seven people.

Carnival time. The lovely ladies representing the United Kingdom of Britain stand in their patriotically decorated carriage. So could this event have occurred at the time of the visit of the Prince and Princess of Wales in 1909? Behind is a strange float with saw blades aloft, perhaps representing industry.

Hawke and Thomas staff have a fashion show, *c.* 1948. It should be noted that the first bikini ever was modelled in Newquay on someone much prettier than Mr Garroway. From left to right these lovely lasses are: -?- , Jack Knight, Mr D.W. Vinall, Ron Taylor, Bill Garroway, Stewart Langmaid. Mr Knight worked for John Julian.

The Carnival Queen in 1936. At the British Legion Annual fete held at Lewennick, courtesy of Mr and Mrs F.W. Baker, Poppy Creighton has just been crowned Carnival Queen by the chairman of the Newquay Urban District Council, Mr R. Sleeman. From left to right: -?-, Miss Stone, Poppy Creighton, Renford Sleeman, Irene Hicks – Miss Newquay, Arthur Bellingham, Betty Rhodda, Pat Morris. The lad in the school cap is John Kennedy.

Polling Day, 1911. The man in the barrow said he would vote for the candidate who provided transport to the poll. The gentlemen with him are: Gould (1), Hedley Westlake (2), Martin Williams (3), Davis (4), Slee (5), Stribley (6), James Vivian (7), -?- (8), Cad Carter Junior (9). The little girl is Audrey Harris.

Charlie Chester, on the right, and Fred Ferrari 'The Voice', on the left, are pictured here in 1949. They pose with two local children, David and Angela Woolf, both feeling thrilled to bits to be pictured with these two top stars.

Kenneth Williams was one of many budding stars who appeared in summer shows in Newquay. He stands on the right, possibly in a play *The Poltergeist* put on in July and August 1948 at the Newquay Theatre in St Michael's Road.

Seven
Newquay People

The premier holiday resort of today, with its railway, large prestigious hotels, shops and services exists because past opportunities were seized and the most made of them. The people, Cornish and upcountry folk, who turned Newquay from a quiet fishing village into a busy town with prospects, were products of Victorian times with all its accompanying vigour, vision and growth. Here we meet some of them and their descendants, through work and play, schools and churches.

Allerina Geziah Tinney was the first baby to be christened in the new St Michael's Chapel of Ease. On the reverse of her portrait it reads 'on the afternoon of October 3rd, 1858'. Her brother Christian Mitchell was also christened that day. The godfathers were Mr I. Moyse and Dick Mitchell.

Mrs Jane Salmon, before she married, became Newquay's first postmistress in 1837. Her salary was £3 3s per annum and in 1842 rose to £5 per year. After twenty-three years and only one more increase in pay, she resigned in 1860. Mrs Salmon excelled in needlework and lace making and can be seen wearing her own hand-made lace collar, which still exists today. She died in 1899, aged eighty-eight.

Madam Hawke, c. 1930. This lady can take credit for establishing the knitwear industry in Newquay. In 1905, upon purchasing a knitting machine, she opened a shop selling knitted hats, suits and coats, eventually supplying Debenham's of London. This London contact led to other factories opening, including one in Crantock Street employing 450 staff. During its heyday the industry provided much needed employment for hundreds of girls. All of this down to one lady and a knitting machine!

Tom Thumb's coachman, with cap in hand, was diminutive Caleb Snell, who lived in a hut at Treloggan, close by the railway line. He had a very loud voice and often frightened local children. General Tom Thumb visited Newquay in 1904.

The Victoria Bingo Hall, in the 1920s. The hall was used for everything from entertainment to furniture sales. Here a fancy dress dance is underway. The hall was also a cinema for many years. In 1926, at a whist tournament and dance, Miss Curtis and Mr Kennedy won a ton of coal. Fortunately they were presented with a voucher and not the actual prize.

Outside the Central Hotel is a group with their hunting dogs, rabbit skins and fish held aloft. The bowler-hatted gentleman, seated centre, is Mr Drew, who was landlord of the Sailor's Arms from 1873 to 1887.

Wesleyan quarterly meeting on the fields below Mount Wise. This was in fact a business meeting!

Tea treat, probably in 1909, for the visit of the Prince and Princess of Wales. Note the size of the buns.

Women's section of the British Legion, formed in the 1920s. They are raising funds by selling produce, including a brace of rabbits. Left to right are: Mrs Button, Mrs Endean, Miss Matheson, Miss Baundy, Miss North, Mrs Fanny Osborne, Mrs Pope, Mrs Inch, Mrs Allen and Clarence Estlick. They also had the use of a shop in Fore Street. The Newquay Electric Light Co. supplied free light and heat, which would not happen today!

Newquay's first fire engine, 1927. From left to right, from the back: Ern Rowe, Bill Cock, Scottie McPherson. Next row: Beadum Billing, Eddie Hoare, Abraham Harris, Freddie Quintrell, Bill Trethewey and Adolphus Bush (standing on the machine). Then there are: Frankie Roberts who delivered the engine, Arch Lukes and Steve Hoare under the ladder. Bottom row: Barber Rickard, Carl Walters (assistant surveyor – later surveyor), Captain Cook, Mr Edmundson, James Vivian (who gave Newquay's Coat of Arms), Hedley Westlake, Bertie Clemens, Fatty Woodward and Roy Trethewey. The boy may be Morley Hocking.

Newquay fire brigade in full dress uniform with the new engine, outside the fire station in Crantock Street.

Newquay post office staff, *c.* 1907. Left to right, standing: ? Williams, Dick Harris, ? Harris, Ferg Hellyer, Eldred Bennett, ? Crawley. W. Ennor is the young lad. Seated: Mrs Harris, Miss Swann, W.R. White (postmaster), Mrs Jacka, Mrs Harris. Front: -?-, Arch Hambly. Another document shows the postmaster as Mr W.R. Wright at Adelaide Place in 1895. White, or Wright, was appointed to his post in 1872.

The last Newquay jouster, George Dungey, *c.* 1900. Jousters sold fish, such as herrings and pilchards around the villages. They each had their own distinctive cry to encourage the housewives to buy. Whether George was the last or not of his kind, he casts an impressive figure.

Captain (R.J.) Jabez Hockin made regular sailings in the 1890s between North and South America and the Mediterranean in a cargo carrying three-masted schooner, the *Julia*. On one trip, to the Gulf of St Lawrence, his ship was trapped in ice floes. He is seen here, in later life, as Newquay's harbour master, with the painting of the cutter *Josephine*. In 1874 carrying coal from Cardiff to Newquay, she and her crew of four, all Hockins, were lost off Trevose Head.

William Furse, a third generation sail maker who came from Mevagissey to Newquay in 1865 and opened a sail-making loft in the Old Malthouse in Beach Road. He remembered the *Banquereau* that was wrecked on Crigga Beach in 1869, with a part cargo of tortoises! For a few years after 1879 he went back to sea, he had been master of the *John Pearce* earlier, and then opened another sail-making concern in Broad Street. The reason that he was photographed with a draughts board was that he was one of the best players in the county.

Newquay Board School II, Crantock Street. The girls' school opened in 1881 and Miss Winter was mistress from then until 1901. In 1893 her salary was £15 a quarter. Treffry Court is on the site now. The Boys' School was a bit further up the road and there was an Infants near the girl's building. From left to right, back row: Miss M. Rodda (teacher), Winnie Stevens, May Clemo, Irene May (Mrs Soloman), Amelia Burt, Lily Westlake, Annie Hugo, Millie Sheppard (Mrs Furse), Maud Sheppard (Mrs Askew), Irene Wendon, Miss Winter (schoolmistress). Third row: Leitha Reynolds, Bessie Rodda, Nellie Rodda, Miss Pascoe (Mrs E. Old), Carrie Hanson (Mrs P. Williams), Miss Ham (Mrs J. Inch), Miss Hugo (Mrs Thompson), Miss Sheppard (Mrs Liddicoat), Miss Irons (Mrs Passmore). Second row: O. Reynolds, Murial Halls, Ethel Farley, Polly Farley, Ursula Edwards, Miss Rowe (Mrs Furse), Nellie Ham, Lily Brown, Miss Carter (Mrs Brown), Miss Veale (Mrs Toms). Front row: Constance Halls, Ethel Currah, Annie Lukes, Winnie Lukes, Miss Williams (Mrs Whitford), Beatrice Soloman, Frances Stevens.

Principal:
OSWALD D. PARKER,
LL.D., B.A., B.Sc. (Lond).

Newquay College, Cornwall, 1903. There were a number of private schools in Newquay for boarders and day pupils. They advertised widely for children. This school was no exception: 'The Ideal Life for Boys. Thorough Tuition for all Examinations amid the happiest and healthiest surroundings. Entire charge of Colonial Pupils. Large Gymnasium and Morris Tube Rifle Range. Chemical Laboratory. Good Sea Bathing and Open-Air Sports. Splendidly situated Fields for Cricket, Football, &c.' The college is now incorporated in the Hotel Bristol, Narrowcliff.

Newquay College, a class in the gymnasium. Note the guns on the racks in the background – for controlling unruly boys?

Walter Murrin outside Island House, Island Crescent, *c.* 1910. This was the home of Dr A.P.G. Hardwick who died in 1954. Walter Murrin, cutting a fine figure, was Hardwick's groom. He arrived in Newquay around 1900 and went on to become a well known builder and developer. He was responsible for part of Island Crescent, villas in the Henver Road and conversions of hotels like the Bella Vista. Penmerrin Court, off Lanhenvor Avenue was recently named after him. 'Pen' was Pengelly, an early partner.

Newquay railway station, 1904. The coachman is Frank Mitchell. His widow, Lottie, in her nineties, was still around in 1982. In the carriage are Dave Old and Will Pearce. The standing gentleman has Headland Hotel blazoned across his hat.

On the beach. Standing on the left is Larry Randall with little Patty Polkinhorne seated beneath her. This delightful scene is a studio photograph with a painted backdrop. Larry's father, G. Randall was master and owner of a beautiful 117 feet long Barquentine *Countess of Devon*. She was too large to get into Newquay Harbour and on several occasions could be seen anchored in the bay. Sadly she was lost with all hands in 1905 on the Great Burbo Bank while taking potter's clay from Poole to Runcorn. Larry was well known for her work through the Red Cross.

Joseph Henwood with his daughter Violet in Berry Road, c. 1910. Mr Henwood used his wagon to transport everything from furniture to parcels and luggage. Most towns had a town porter with vehicle.

Staffieri's ice cream van, c. 1950. Augustine and Theresa Staffieri came from Italy and started their ice cream business in Newquay around 1904. They had concessions from the local council to sell ice cream on the beaches in summer. Sadly, Mr Staffieri was killed on 13 September 1918 at the last battle of the Somme. His son, Pip, was born the month before and this lively and active octogenarian still lives in the same house he was born in. The family supplied the summer theatres with ices in the intermissions and, before the days of refrigerators, the hotels, on a daily basis. The little girl, leaning on the Morris van may be Margaret Mitchelmore.

Dr Arthur Hardwick MD mixed his own medicines, pulled teeth without gas and held the post of Newquay's Medical Officer of Health. Interested in the weather he was a Fellow of the Royal Meteorological Society. Here he is at Newquay's meteorological station behind Prospect House, East Street.

Dr Boyle dropped dead in the street in 1888. His obituary read 'Our much beloved, highly respected townsman Thomas Boyle, Surgeon'. He came to Newquay around 1856. A curious story is told of him. Late one night while returning from Porth, across the Barrowfields, a large setter dog joined him and licked his hand. Suddenly from the darkness, two men appeared and demanded his watch and purse. He refused to give them up and said that at the drop of his hand the dog would jump at the throat of one of them. The dog began to growl and the men left. It walked all the way with the doctor to Newquay and then left him. He never saw the dog again!

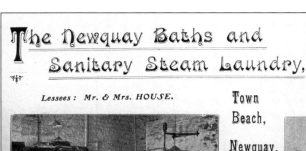

The Newquay Baths and Sanitary Steam Laundry,

Lessees : Mr. & Mrs. HOUSE.

Town Beach, Newquay.

The steam laundry and baths had this advertisement in the Mates Guide of 1903. Here Towan Beach is called 'Town' Beach, still called thus by older inhabitants.

Newquay steam laundry staff, c. 1903. Some of the women are pictured in spotless aprons. They were kept very busy, especially with all the linen from the hotels that needed washing and starching. The particular position filled by the dog is not known.

John Hoyte's removal van, and staff with John Hoyte in his bowler hat and suit, and his wife to the right. They had the contract to supply horses for the town bus, the lifeboat, the tram track trucks, the harbour and at Fowey Docks. Their first stables were on the Whim. An early horse-drawn bus service run by Mrs Hoyte included a route to Truro and was used on market days to take produce there. However, passengers had to get off the bus and walk if there was a big hill en route. She also carried cash, perhaps £2,000 at a time hidden in a basket. The money was collected from a bank in Truro and used to pay herring fishermen and helpers in Newquay.

Newquay gasworks staff. Stan Jennings is the man on the far right. The gasworks was on Tolcarne Farm land, by the railway station, between it and Tolcarne Road. This was Avondale Road in the 1900s and past where Albany Road starts there is still a terrace of houses, known as Trocadero, built on a curve which housed gas workers.

Henry Martyn general and builders merchants was a business dealing in manure, corn, coal, slate etc. based at Trevemper. Henry took over from Silas E. Martyn and other Martyns were involved with the business, which started in 1806. Martyns were yeomen farmers and owned Penpol, Tregunnel and Trevithick. During the time of the schooners, goods like coal, off loaded at Penpol Creek would be carried up river to Trevemper Bridge by barges. The coming of the railways revolutionised this. Martyn's Stores was up the hill from Trevemper Bridge, going towards Treloggan Industrial Estate and some of the buildings still remain, part fire damaged.

Martyn's lorry at Penhallow Cottage, the old chapel, Trevemper, *c*. 1930. Wearing the cap is William John Dunsford Stephens, the driver, and standing on the right is his younger brother, Rex. The lorry is a Model T Ford with solid tyres.

Sir Richard Tangye, 1905. He bought Glendorgal, near Porth in 1882. Born in Illogan, with his brothers he went to Birmingham, where they founded the very successful engineering firm in the Tangye name. It was noted for the good relationship between the shop floor and boardroom, unusual in those times. In 1863 they built 'Cornubia', a road locomotive which travelled at 20 miles per hour. An Act of Parliament stopping vehicles from travelling at more than 4 miles per hour was made because of their engine, putting back the use of steam driven road transport for many years. He died in 1906 aged seventy-three.

Glendorgal, 1903. The lady on the left, standing in front of Harry Tangye's Panhard is Nigel Tangye's mother. She had three children, Colin, Derek and Nigel. Derek and Nigel were both authors of renown.

Nigel Tangye FRGS, born 1909, stands afore the *Johann Carl* at Porth. Nigel Tangye, a Cornishman, was an author and hotelier. He wrote on diverse themes, including the *Story of Glendorgal*. He was a man of learning and great charm. He turned the Glendorgal into a hotel of note in 1951. The *Johann Carl*, a German built boat, was bought by Alexander Stephens in 1899. Taking china clay from Newquay to Bristol, she was lost in the Bristol Channel in 1917. Her master, J. Billing Senior, drowned.

E. J. Ennor, Bard Barth Enor, respected local historian and a past President of the Newquay Old Cornwall Society in 1932, was a member of a well known Newquay family. He served on the UDC for eighteen years and was chairman from 1932 to 1934. As an architect and surveyor he was responsible for many buildings in Newquay. He was steward to the Cardell estate and surveyor to the Stephens who owned Porth Veor.

C.R. Bellingham was a successful builder in Newquay, c. 1900. He was, as a young man with John Ennor, apprenticed to Richard Carne who was responsible for much building in the town including the Wesleyan chapel. Mr Bellingham lived in Clarence Villa, Fore Street. Perhaps his most notable construction was the Hotel Victoria built in 1897.

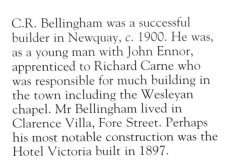

Gannel Shipyard, below Tregunnel, *c.* 1877. The yard was started by Thomas Clemens around 1839. By 1877 the third generation of Clemens', Thomas and John, ran the operation. This schooner is the *Louise*, being built for R. Chegwidden and R.J. Hockin, local men. Her hull was 87 feet and 4 inches long. She had a semi-elliptical stern and a three-quarter woman figurehead. In 1937, after a long career, her hull became a breakwater at Falmouth. Behind the *Louise*, can be seen the long steam box, where timbers were placed so they could be softened and then curved to fit the shape of the ship.

The *Louise* at sea. She was launched from the Gannel Shipyard in February 1877. Vessels built at the yard had to be launched at high water on a spring tide. This had to be done broadside on, so must have caused a spectacular splash. They were then towed round to the harbour for fitting out. As with most Newquay vessels, she was registered at Padstow. Her captain, R. Chegwidden, lived at Belmont Place, Newquay.

The Old Farmhouse, Pentire was the home of the Pascoe family, with Dr Dick its head. He was not really a doctor but he was a character. In August 1908, he put an advert in the local paper to exchange his fourteen-month-old heifer and a three-month-old yearling for a good dairy cow. It is not known whether he was successful.

Dr Dick's farmyard at Pentire. This is a wonderful picture of a jumble of chickens and pigs, scratching around, with the heifer pondering the scene.

Henry Salmon. The Salmon family lived at Trevemper for so long that there is a lane named after them, linking their farm with the river Gannel. This venerable old gentlemen is Mr Henry Salmon, photographed at Trevemper Mill. In 1851 the miller was Constantine House.

Wesley church opening on Friday 8 July 1904. Under the strong leadership of the Reverend and Mrs Hodgson Smith, the congregation enthusiastically raised money, making every stage of the building an 'event'. A remarkable feature of this church is the organ, built for the parish church of Andover over 200 years ago. Though rebuilt and modified a number of times, some of the original Snetzler pipes still exist.

St Michael's church was needed because the original St Michael's Chapel of Ease, where Woolworths now is in Bank Street, was getting too small. Land was obtained in Marcus Hill and fund raising commenced. The foundation stone was laid on 7 September 1911. The views show part of the procession of priests and St Michael's choir on the day.

The consecration of St Michael's church took place in 1911. The tower was added in 1967.

Jingles waiting in Central Square. Perhaps they are waiting for 'chucking out' time at the Central Inn, on the left. Jingles could be hired, like modern day taxis. They had side facing seats and were licensed. There is also a pram in the picture, even these had similar springing to some horse-drawn vehicles.

Penpol ferry, c. 1914. The passengers are Eveline and Frank Clifton, later Mrs Guy Peirson and Colonel Clifton, grandchildren of old Colonel Trish, known in Newquay eighty years ago. The villa on the left was the first to be built on Pentire. Note the life jacket and hat worn by the oarsman, pushing out the boat for the perilous journey. In fact the river Gannel can be dangerous and has claimed several lives over the centuries.

Newquay United Band Of Hope formed in the early 1900s. Pictured are: W. Oxenberry, Bill Wilts, W. Henwood, L. Vivian, Sid Flamank, Ed Trethewey, J. Nicholas, Harold Hugo, Ern Barberry (bandmaster), Joe Emmett, Stan Flamanck, Percy Burt, John Pengelly, E. Martin, Stan Rawlings, Hugh Robertson, John Curry, ? Slocombe.

The Volunteers Band, Light Infantry Newquay. Brass bands and Cornwall go together like clotted cream, splits and jam.

Eight
Memorable Events

Newquay has its share of memorable events. Some end in mourning and others in celebration. Some are just plain curious!

The Headland Riots occurred on 31 August 1897, when townsfolk destroyed a wooden hut erected in Little Fistral Meadow, at the beginning of construction of the Headland Hotel. There was a Dutch auction and building materials and bits of hut ended up over the cliff. Local people had had enough of losing rights of access and common land used for centuries for drying nets, sheep grazing and collecting beach sand and such like. Results of their handiwork, a pile of planks and wheel barrows, are here being viewed a day or so later. Twenty-one men were charged with causing malicious damage to Headland Hotel Company property. They were found guilty and fined £2 each. There was a positive outcome to the riot. The hotel was built, after a delay to allow the fuss to die down, and remaining land on the Headland was leased to the council for ninety-nine years on the understanding that no further buildings, roads and fences be allowed. This meant plans for new housing estates were scrapped!

Outside John Cotton's chapel, 1897. The solicitor's clerk from Plymouth takes evidence from the men involved in the Headland Riots. Seated at the table from left to right: Uncle Jim Clemens, Nick Hocking, William Carter and William Pappin and the clerk. From left to right, standing: Rubin Trethewey, William Cook, Billy Matthews, R.J. Hocking, Dick Hocking, Sid Trewerry, Charlie Chegwidden, Will James, Captain Bellamy, Captain Prout, Steve Hoare, Will Stephens. Seated on the wall are: Bert Clemens, Lou Gill, Ned Trebilcock.

Headland Hotel opened in 1900. Here work is finally getting under way. Note the steam engine in the background. After the riots the Urban District Council stopped building going ahead by removing planning permission on the grounds that the drains were faulty. Six months later they reversed their decision.

The north wall of the harbour was breached by a great gale in 1889. About fifty feet of wall collapsed. Masonry was loosened for about one hundred feet. Luckily the vessels in the harbour survived the storm. That year it was used by 107 ships. In all there were 70 seafaring families in the town.

Royal visit. Newquay has had a long association with royalty. The bunting is out for the visit of the Prince and Princess of Wales to Newquay in 1909. Fore street looks its finest with red, white and blue decorations decking the street.

Royal visit, 1909. The Prince of Wales, wearing the bowler, has just inspected the *James Stevens* No. 5 lifeboat. The gentlemen at the front, boaters in hand, are Alex Stephens of Porth on the left and Mr R. Hawkey on the right.

Mr James Carne of St Columb Minor waits to meet the Prince and Princess of Wales in 1909. He had achieved much fame because of his age – 103 – and his long service as St Columb Minor parish clerk.

Tea treat. Newquay children have tea and buns in memory of the visit of the Prince and Princess of Wales in 1909. The party was held in the fields below Mount Wise.

The Princes Edward and Albert in 1911. Here they are on a visit to the Headland Hotel. Mr Joos, in the doorway, was the manager. He was a rather rotund German. The boys visited Glendorgal on another outing and Mrs Trembath the housekeeper wrote about this. She noted that the boys spent some time playing with a weighing machine, getting on it separately and together, and wondering how many of them it would take to weigh as much as Mr Joos.

Sir Hugh Protheroe Smith, Chief Constable of Cornwall, was host to the Princes; Henry, Duke of Gloucester and George, Duke of Kent in 1913, recuperating from whooping cough. His home was Pentowan in Newquay.

Wreck of the *Bessie*, 1912. The vessel, bound for Penryn from Cork with a cargo of oats, went ashore by Bothwicks Rocks, Towan Island. Captain Tabb mistook the lights of Newquay for St Ives. The crew of four and a dog were rescued by the Rocket Brigade who lowered ropes over the cliff and pulled all to safety. The one sad fatality was Mrs Flamank, who fell over the cliff while watching the rescue. Her body was not found until two hours later.

Salving the oats at Newquay, 1912. Local people doing a bit of 'wrecking', salvaging *Bessie*'s cargo. Wrecking in this context simply meant collecting up the goods that ended up on beaches after storms and taking them to a safer place!

HMS *Monarch* funeral A dreadful accident occurred on Thursday 25 June 1914, resulting in the deaths of Hugh McAdam Bradrick, Gilbert Frances Wallis and Walter Lupton, all seventeen years old. When hoisting in a launch onto the HMS *Monarch* in a swelling sea, a shackle broke and they were struck on their heads with a block, suffering fatal injuries.

HMS *Monarch* funeral procession. On the Saturday the funeral was held for Bradrick and Lupton at Crantock Street Cemetery. Wallis' body was sent by rail to his family. The whole event was marked by a procession from the harbour to the cemetery headed by the Band of the HMS *Monarch*. Some 500 Navy personnel attended. Several thousands of people respectfully witnessed this sad event.

Recruiting march, 16 May 1915 in East Street. A young man wishing to enlist would fall in and march with the rest. Five men in civvies can be seen near the front. This must have been a stirring sight to all those who witnessed it.

Newquay Isolation Hospital was opened in 1907, at Trevenson, now the site of the council rubbish tip. The staff and patients from left to right are: -?-, Pol Pearce (with well wrapped infant) and John Rowe standing next to Granny Williams. She and her husband were the caretakers, later succeeded by Mr Collyer. The conditions were fairly primitive as there was no internal water supply to start with. Nobody would forget a stay here!

The SS *War Grange* was torpedoed seven miles off Newquay on 15 May 1918. The explosion rent a great hole in her side and five of her crew died. A Newquay lifeboat stood by while the *War Grange* was towed onto Towan Beach, patched up and towed away to be torpedoed again. In St Michael's church a brass plaque reads 'In Memory of Frank Selby – 1st Engineer, Walter Klotz – 2nd Engineer, John Appleby – 3rd Engineer, James Cunningham Man – Cabin Boy, Abdul Mahjed – Donkeyman'.

The SS *War Grange* showing the damage to her side. In 1995 shifting sands on Towan Beach revealed a large piece of twisted metal discarded during repairs. A danger to bathers, it was cut up on the beach and removed.

Hotel Edgecumbe fire, 1919. The hotel caught fire at 2 a.m. in the morning. Luckily, Arthur Byford, sleeping near the kitchen, smelled burning. He called the boots and they found the kitchen a mass of flames. The only casualty was a guest who jumped out of a window, breaking an ankle. Everyone else escaped by walking out into the wind and rain in their night clothes, at the calm insistence of Nellie Dorset and Mary James. The manageress, Miss Strutt, had time to call her dog and have it muzzled before it left the premises, as 'there was certain to be a policeman outside'.

Hotel Edgecumbe fire. The fire was indeed a spectacular sight and people came in their hundreds to see the blaze and its aftermath. The hotel was fully insured and damage amounted to about £10,000. This, of course, did not include the expensive jewellery and luggage of the guests.

F.W. Woolworth's began to acquire land for their new shop. The coming of Woolworth's caused a great deal of talk in town.

St Michael's Chapel of Ease being demolished, c. 1938. The original chapel was built in 1858. When it was finally sold to F.W. Woolworth and Co. Ltd, the Women's Institute were the owners, they had had it from 1922. Though not in use as a church for many years, it was still a great loss to Newquay people.

Nine
Newquay's Beaches

Newquay's extensive sandy bathing beaches have always been a major attraction for the town. First it was a demure dip for health reasons and nobody sunbathed. By the 1920s surfing was the vogue. The boards were wooden and there was not a wet suit in sight.

Newquay railway station, 1903. A huge swarm of visitors depart from the station to enjoy some time in the prestigious resort of Newquay, famous for its beaches. They will promenade, take charabanc trips or sit on the beach in deckchairs. They may even bathe in the sea! What is also of note in this view is the framework for the gasometer, between the station buildings and houses on the left. The gasworks date from 1886.

Towan Beach, Newquay, August 1907. It must have been a sunny day as the children on the donkeys are wearing their hats. Donkey rides, Punch and Judy and other popular entertainment, including concerts, kept the holidaymakers amused. The original canvas covered 'Cosy Nook' can be seen on the promenade at the back of the beach. Seating was deck chairs. This was eventually replaced by a permanent building which closed in 1993.

The Newquay Steam Laundry & Baths Co., Towan beach, was opened in October 1895 by Mrs Michael Williams, wife of the company's chairman. She ceremoniously turned on the 'tap' to what was the first steam laundry in Cornwall. Water was available for the works from a mine adit behind the buildings in the cliff. Next to the laundry was Gover and Sherwill's Mineral Water Factory. There were many complaints, even then, about siting these businesses here, especially when the laundry chimney was belching out great volumes of smoke and steam.

Towan Beach, *c.* 1915. A typical Edwardian beach scene. The town council had by now bought the foreshore from high to low water mark, extending from the North Pier of the harbour to the edge of Tolcarne Beach, from the Duchy of Cornwall. It also acquired the Steam Laundry at the back of Towan Beach, converting some of the buildings to shelters, erected the iron railings and laid down the public promenade to a width of forty feet. The canvas covered Cosy Nook provided concerts in the summer and there was a rifle range.

Bathing machines, Towan Beach, *c.* 1915. Young men make sand castles and one has his towel rolled up under his arm. Bathing in sea water was thought to be good for the health. The bathing machines, for changing in, would be moved up or down relative to the water's edge so one could use them to enter and exit the water without so much as a bare ankle being seen! On the left is the harbour. On the Headland can be seen the Atlantic Hotel and to the right, the last remaining Huer's House in Newquay.

Nannies and their charges enjoy Newquay's beaches, *c.* 1911. Many wealthy families came to Newquay for the summer, taking over whole houses. They brought their staff and of course nanny to look after the children.

Newquay postcard. This seems to be an unusual view of Tolcarne Beach, pictured before any permanent beach huts were erected.

Fistral Beach, with the Headland Hotel in the background, 1903. This view is only part of a much larger beach, now world famous as a surfing venue. The rocky cliff behind the beach is now mostly covered in blown sand.

Watergate Bay, with a group of holidaymakers shrimping, c. 1900. Watergate Bay Hotel is in the distance. The hotel's telegram address was 'Sunshine, St Columb Minor'. It had a garage, stored petrol and had an inspection pit in common with many of the other large hotels. Perhaps this reflects how unreliable the early motor cars were.

Newquay's beaches, sometime after 1931. A wonderful aerial view of Great Western and Tolcarne Beach and the railway station. With the Atlantic ocean rollers as a backdrop, bathing huts are now used as changing rooms rather than for preserving modesty. Surfing has already begun in Newquay, with wooden boards and the ladies wearing rubber bathing caps. The railway station is very busy, bringing holidaymakers and day trippers to town.

Ten
Out of Town

As Newquay has expanded, its boundaries have absorbed farms, hamlets and villages. Many still retain their old 'worlde' charm.

Porth Veor, home of the Stephens family, *c*. 1890. After the Arundells of Lanherne, the Stephens were the next important owners of Porth Veor. The family had held a lease there since 1770 and Ephraim Stephens purchased the holding in 1825. He also bought Glendorgal and sold it to Sir Francis Rodd. The next time we meet a member of the family, it is William Stephens, who keeps a diary and writes 'Poor Mark Cardell committed a sad act by shooting himself in a barn at Trenance part of his face and an eye shot away'. This was on 7 October 1853. The barn was up by Trenance Lane which is called Marcus Hill today. This is because Mark was said to have rode down the hill after his accident. William Stephens married Lucy Ann Bailey and they had two sons, William John and Alexander, and five daughters. The eldest boy was Dr Willie Stephens, local physician and amateur historian, who died as the result of a car accident in 1948. The younger, Alexander was born a year later than William, in 1867. The family were becoming more successful and in 1884 the stylish villa Porth Veor was built; now a hotel. By 1890 the family had bought their first schooner, the *Engineer*, and Alex Stephens was its manager. She was needed for the family business which made the Stephens the principal merchants of Porth. They dealt in coal, manure and other goods.

The five Stephens sisters, *c.* 1950. Left to right, standing: Ruth, Lucy (who married Colonel Rusher), and Mary. Kneeling: Margaret, and Elizabeth (who married Lancelot Henry). Margaret died aged ninety-eight, at Hayne in Newquay – the family home – in 1962. Elizabeth lived at Gwenna Cottage, Porth Beach Road, with her lighting and cooking fuelled by paraffin.

The *Engineer* and *Heather Bell* moored in Porth estuary. Trevelgue Head, also known as Porth Island, shows the harbour that was built in the 1870s by Pendarves Vivian for his steam yacht. He was an MP of Place, St Anthony and owned the land on which the Glendorgal Hotel sits. To the left is a cutting in the cliff which passes through a shillet bank constructed 2,000 years ago. The *Heather Bell* was built at Cardigan in 1873 and registered at Padstow from 1888 until 1905. The sloop *Engineer* was owned by the Stephens of Porth. In 1897 while bringing manure from Cork to Porth she was lost at Park Head and only the body of the mate, T. Hocking, was ever found.

Mr Hocking farming at Porth. Backed by the Porth estuary and Trevelgue Head, famous for its Iron Age remains of settlement and iron smelting, the hay is being brought in. Just behind the cart is Concord Fish Cellar and sheds used for storing coal, brought in by sailing vessels.

St Columb Minor Sunday school, c. 1900. The Wesleyan Sunday school tea treat is enjoyed by everyone, all are dressed in their best. When Newquay was just a scattering of houses, St Columb Minor was the nearest village.

The Farmer's Arms, St Columb Minor, caught fire on 13 October 1888. Here work is being done to repair it. The fire was started accidently when a sparkler fell on the roof. Three little boys were involved, Ross Currah, Silas ? and Alec Sneddon. They were only about seven years old. Ross lit a sparkler. As it flared he panicked, ran into the middle of the road and threw it up into the air. It didn't come down, so Silas shouted to a man called Arthur Roberts. Mr Roberts said 'That one's in the thatch, boy'. He told the landlord, Samuel Argall, but the customers said the roof was too wet to cause trouble! Within ten minutes the thatch was in flames.

This little bridge has disappeared under a tarmac road leading to a double roundabout, at the bottom of Trenance Hill. Some of the old buildings in the background thankfully still exist today and are now known as Trenance Cottages. To the left of the gentleman with the dog there is now a lovely rose garden. Today the stream is trapped within man-made banks and leads down to the boating lakes.

Trenance Cottage. Just up the lane from where the previous picture was taken this cottage was demolished in 1927. It was the home of Mr and Mrs Simon Trebilcock. In 1925 the clerk to Newquay Town Council was instructed 'to negotiate with elderly Mr Trebilcock terms of a new tenancy on his delivering vacant possession of his cottage at Trenance'. The cottage was declared unfit to live in, due to the poor water supply. This was followed by much debate in the Town Council as to whether the house could be made fit again but it was demolished.

River Gannel, *c.* 1906. Villas were being built on the Newquay side of the river for private residents and visitors. The first big house was probably for Miss Michell of the Fort. The Gannel has two 'unique' features. One is the Gannel Bore, a great tidal wave last recorded in 1893. Then there is the Gannel Crake, a fabled beast, never seen, but with a cry to put the fear of death in your heart! It haunts the river especially at dawn and dusk, around the Penpol and Trethellan area. You have been warned!

Trevemper Mill. Up the River Gannel, at the highest point of the tide, are a packhorse bridge originating in the 1600s and a modern road bridge, side by side. Just beyond were the buildings, including Trevemper Mill, shown on the right. On the left next to the miller's thatched house is the 'salt house'. Sadly the buildings were demolished after a fire gutted the family home in 1963.

The Ship Inn, Crantock, in the 1890s. The inn was built in the mid-1600s with a huge thatched roof. The left-hand side was destroyed in a fire around 1900 and rebuilt with a slate roof. The inn closed in 1870. The proprietor in 1840 was Henry Crocker, who was also a carpenter. A.O. Crowle says of it 'Haunt of Sailors, carters, smugglers'. There is said to be a tunnel under the building. In the eighteenth century the notorious 'Crantock Games' were held here. No-one seems to know what they were but they were notorious! The first school, run by Miss Teague Husband, was in a room here. The brewhouse to the inn was demolished in 1892.

St Crantock's Well and the old cottages opposite the Ship Inn, c. 1915. The old gentleman on the left is probably Mr Thomas Harris, Mrs A.L. Stevenson's great-grandfather. He died in 1917 aged ninety-seven. Her grandparents lived in the cottage behind the well and brought up nine children before moving to Pentire Farm, across the Gannel. The phaeton is Dr Hardwicks and Walter Murrin is the groom.

The Round House, Crantock. This gives an idea of what rural life was really like in the past. Instead of cars there are cattle. Crantock village is surrounded by farms and many of its older houses were farmhouses. The Round House is just beyond the Ship Inn. Inside was a horse whim. Between the inn and the Round House is a courtyard, at the back of which is a converted 400-year-old farm building, now selling quality crafts.

Just a line from Newquay.